Animals and Their Senses

ANIMAL SMELL

by Kirsten Hall

Reading consultant: Susan Nations, M.Ed.,
author/literacy coach/consultant

WEEKLY READER
EARLY LEARNING LIBRARY

Please visit our web site at: www.earlyliteracy.cc
For a free color catalog describing Weekly Reader® Early Learning Library's list
of high-quality books, call 1-877-445-5824 (USA) or 1-800-387-3178 (Canada).
Weekly Reader® Early Learning Library's fax: (414) 336-0164.

Library of Congress Cataloging-in-Publication Data

Hall, Kirsten.
    Animal smell / Kirsten Hall.
        p. cm. — (Animals and their senses)
    Includes bibliographical references and index.
    ISBN 0-8368-4804-7 (lib. bdg.)
    ISBN 0-8368-4810-1 (softcover)
    1. Smell—Juvenile literature.   I. Title.
    QP458.H315   2005
    573.8'77—dc22   2005046177

This North American edition first published in 2006 by
Weekly Reader® Early Learning Library
A Member of the WRC Media Family of Companies
330 West Olive Street, Suite 100
Milwaukee, WI 53212 USA

Copyright © 2006 by Nancy Hall, Inc.

Weekly Reader® Early Learning Library Editor: Barbara Kiely Miller
Weekly Reader® Early Learning Library Art Direction: Tammy West
Weekly Reader® Early Learning Library Graphic Designer and Page Layout: Jenni Gaylord

Photo Credits
The publisher would like to thank the following for permission to reproduce their royalty-free photographs:
AbleStock: Cover, 4, 5, 6, 8, 10, 12, 20; Corel: 11; Digital Vision: 14, 15, 16, 17, 18, 21; Fotosearch/
Brand X Pictures: Title page, 9, 13; Fotosearch/Digital Vision: 7; Fotosearch/image 100: 19

Printed in the United States of America

1 2 3 4 5 6 7 8 9 09 08 07 06 05

Note to Educators and Parents

Reading is such an exciting adventure for young children! They are beginning to integrate their oral language skills with written language. To encourage children along the path to early literacy, books must be colorful, engaging, and interesting; they should invite the young reader to explore both the print and the pictures.

Animals and Their Senses is a new series designed to help children read about the five senses in animals. In each book young readers will learn interesting facts about the bodies of some animals and how the featured sense works for them.

Each book is specially designed to support the young reader in the reading process. The familiar topics are appealing to young children and invite them to read — and reread — again and again. The full-color photographs and enhanced text further support the student during the reading process.

In addition to serving as wonderful picture books in schools, libraries, homes, and other places where children learn to love reading, these books are specifically intended to be read within an instructional guided reading group. This small group setting allows beginning readers to work with a fluent adult model as they make meaning from the text. After children develop fluency with the text and content, the book can be read independently. Children and adults alike will find these books supportive, engaging, and fun!

— Susan Nations, M.Ed., author, literacy coach, and consultant in literacy development

People use their noses to smell.
Scents, or smells, are carried through the air. They enter the holes in our noses, or **nostrils**, when we breathe.

Flowers and warm cookies have good smells. Dirty sneakers and garbage have bad smells.

Most kinds of animals smell with their noses, too. A polar bear can smell **prey** even in the snow.

A squirrel buries nuts and seeds in the ground. It uses its sense of smell to find them again.

trunk

An elephant's nostrils are at the end of its trunk. An elephant remembers other elephants by their scents.

A hippo can smell the air even when it swims. Its nose often stays above the water.

A shark has small nostrils, but it has a strong sense of smell. It can smell other animals that are far away.

A wolf can smell better than a shark can. A wolf can smell a deer across a huge forest.

A cat has an excellent sense of smell. It can smell about fourteen times better than a human can.

A dog can smell many things that people cannot smell. Some dogs can follow scents that are days old.

A lizard does not smell with its nostrils. It smells with the **roof**, or top, of its mouth.

tongue

A snake also smells with the roof of its mouth. First, it grabs scents from the air with its tongue.

Ants use smells to tell each other things.
They find food by following scents left
behind by other ants.

hive

Bees also use smells to tell each other
things. Honeybees give off different
scents. They use the scents to know
what jobs they should do in the hive.

An eel must use its sense of smell when it hunts. Eels cannot see very well.

Moles cannot see well, either. Like an eel, a mole uses its sense of smell to find food.

Many animals have strong scents. They sniff each other to find out if they are from the same family.

Many animals use their sense of smell
when they hunt for food. Smells also
warn animals of danger and help them
stay alive in the wild.

Glossary

hive — a home for honeybees

nostrils — the outer openings of the nose

prey — animals that are hunted and killed by other animals for food

scents — certain smells or odors

For More Information

Books

Animal Noses. Look Once, Look Again (series). David M. Schwartz (Gareth Stevens)

Animal Senses. Spyglass Books (series). Janine Scott and Joan Steward (Compass Point Books)

Animal Talk: How Animals Communicate Through Sight, Sound, and Smell. Animal Behavior (series). Etta Kaner (Kids Can Press)

Smelling in Living Things. Karen Hartley, Chris Macro, and Philip Taylor (Heinemann Library)

Web Sites

Noses and Other Things That Smell
www.andrewlost.com/sense_of_smell_k1.htm
Animals that use unusual body parts to smell with

23

Index

About the Author

Kirsten Hall is an author and editor. While she was still in high school, she published her first book for children, *Bunny, Bunny*. Since then she has written and published more than eighty titles. A former teacher, Kirsten currently spends her days writing and editing and her evenings tutoring. She lives in New York City with her husband.